THESE POEMS ARE ___ tone, at moments enigmatic. They move wonderfully in and out of figurative flight and let plain statement take over in unexpected places, often turning up a surprise topic. They don't pretend not to suffer, but they don't brood. Cued by its title, this collection explores everything implied in Stevens's "I wish that I might be a thinking stone." Etched by thinking, here is an aesthetic to offset chagrin and disappointment, aging, and sympathies with other beings that would otherwise be too intense.

    Paul Fry

WHAT I LOVE—and there are so many things to love—most about Lauri Robertson's *An Aesthetic of Stone* is how wildly abandoned it is, how funny it is, and how—in poem after poem—one senses a wholly new way how rumination works and shows us how we negotiate who we are, what we have lost and where we stand, particularly in this exact and fragile time of being alive. There are, also, in this wonderful first collection, so many ways of inventing the truth, along with so many voices to get us there. They are hard won poems, of course, but they are written down with such a shameless sense of wonder, that I couldn't stop being surprised. Happy and surprised.

    Michael Klein

...MUCH TO ADMIRE...THOUGHTFUL, FULL OF BREATH and affection for the details that populate a life.

    Elaina Ellis

An Æsthetic of Stone

Lauri Robertson

SPUYTEN DUYVIL
New York City

© 2020 Lauri Robertson

ISBN 978-1-952419-07-2

Cover photo by the author: "Chenonceau 2020"

Library of Congress Control Number: 2020934218

FOR DAVID

Contents

About Life

It's never right.
Someone's heart is always heavy.
Someone just had to put their dog down
and water is springing from their eyes like a plague of grasshoppers.

Someone feels guilty for not being able to help
and someone would never consider helping anyone
ever.

Someone's annoying you with a poem that's just a list.

My husband doesn't like lists. I think he thinks
it's a cheap way to use the language. (Plus he hates, especially
to-do lists.)

But, back to the subject. (I'm allowed to wander because I'm old
and, like an old dog, have been good for a long time.)

Because it's never right
we had to put our dog down last week. Her name was Maddie.
My husband took her for a last ride through the moors.
(How grateful I am to have a husband.)

The next day, unbeknownst to me, he went back
and called her name, and called and called
and no dog came.

We (Americans) have taken to saying *wabi-sabi*
believing it means tolerance
of impermanence and imperfection.
(Does it seem strange we think of *Japanese*
as nearly synonymous with perfection?)

We know we'll be following the dog—*good dog Maddie*—
and our friends will. Some already have.
We just don't know when.
But, at a certain age, we know it's the end
of immortality.

We know our lives are not worth the anxiety spent on them.
(And yet, we're still anxious.)
We know that simple language is best, sometimes.
We know thought is not simple, and language is a pale
rider to describe it. We know it's not about language anyway
not at all.

We know bewilderment, and we know gratitude
for crazy keening in the moors.

An Æsthetic of Stone

To simplify, yes, to be
rock solid, a wall.

Not mystical, no, not *a stone*
or what you can't get blood from.

Not, in particular, found in a riverbed
though there are signs—stigmata of coquina.

But quarried, with striations
beyond imagination of how it was done
back when.

To simplify, first and foremost
texture without pattern
shadow without color
or a little of these, subtle
heavy, slow.

To simplify
years of inchoate longing.
Now simply the light
across a wall.

Hot in the sun, cool in the shade
wet with mossy invasion
eroded as if Medieval steps
or by lips
on the foot of a saint.

ANDALUSIA

The olive trees were singing to me
and stood upright on the crooked land
or more or less, and gracefully
or leaning gracefully—is it too trite to say
like dancers—with soft lace falling, or tears.

A land so unmistakable—
beatifically tortuous hills
foreign to me as God.

Yet, in the incomprehensible
in a herd of happy young bulls
a visceral sense of honoring them
even in their impending deaths
especially in their deaths.

In the red of the cloth—*muleta*—their blood
and ours, and I was terrified to think
I almost understood.

As If

Once upon a time
in psychoanalytic land
there was a personality called *as if.*

No *there,* there. Just the desire, perhaps
and the fiction. But, who
behind the curtain? *Are you nobody, too?*

How privileged do you want
to be, how lettered, decent
or extremely, obscenely wealthy?

Why live by a normopathic checklist
a false self with none true to cue?
How do you decide what's a worthy goal anyway?

My grade school friends once said
I'd imitate the walls if I could
as I cultivated a cursive writing affectation—

They were being mean, although it was also
just an observation. But, it's useful
to try on an identity to see if it fits

to play with *as if* as long as
the socially competent puppeteer
exists.

What *do* you want?
As if having what you want
is the right thing, or right.

What do I want?

To be neither leader nor follower
to *belong*, as if
we're a good species.

BIRTHDAY POEM

From the bedroom window
a good ways away, every morning
two birds poke in and out
of two chimney pots.

Inexplicable, my love for them
the raw glee, eye-opening anticipation
the concern.

I assume they're a couple—
large birds, quite black
or silhouetted as such
some kind of raven, or crow
research fails to reveal.

One large, one smaller chimney pot
in and out, hippity-hop
atop the Ambassador's house.

(He is elderly and kind, as is his wife.
Their house is huge, and shabby.
They walk slowly, and we worry.)

How truly strange to live
on a rim of terracotta.

Every morning I make sure
there are two birds there.
What if one fell into the stack overnight?

After all, didn't our chimney sweep
who arrived Dickensian brush and all
find a dead bird in the flue?
(Ooh, my shoulders are in pain with the thought
of being unable to flutter.)

Worry is a terrible thing, although my point
is primordial delight.

I presume baby birds will appear one day
as soon as spring is soon
but eschew sentiment, even for life going on
even after the elderly couple will be gone.
(Should we bother making friends with them?)

Not about sentiment
but an unrepresentable state of joy.

How they draw me every morning
to lift the thin curtains
to see clearly, to count
to breathe.

Deprived Children in My Neighborhood...

...is the title of story I didn't write a quarter of a century ago
about a memory from a quarter of a century earlier still.
I don't know why it was *children,* plural—I was thinking of one girl.

Her name may have been Caroline. I didn't know her
but the story was really about the inadequacy of memory—
shadowy, oddly specific, persistent.

She lived next door, or rather, in a real house adjacent to our apartment
building
in the large wooded lot before they built a huge, ugly, modern thing with
terraces
where all the flight attendants stayed.

She had straight black hair, and her father was a doctor. Or maybe
he was her uncle. Maybe there was no mother. Or a mother conflated
with a gypsy I once saw in France.

There was an explosion and a fire. A childhood friend remembers the
cinders.
There was something about drugs. The doctor went to jail.

My father once found a robin's egg on the property. I want to say it was
whole
that we kept it warm, and a baby bird appeared. But, it was a broken
shell—
an enchanted blue I'd never seen before invented the world.

I remember her tangled black hair, and her dirty arms.

One day someone came to our door collecting for "deprived children".
"I'm a deprived child," I said, a little kittenishly. There was a smile
before my father interrupted. *But, was I?*

I remember our darkish hallway, the between-the-wars brass banisters
I slid down like an acrobat, terrazzo floors etched by yet
another half a century—the persistence of architecture.

I was not lonely or hungry or cold. The hapless mother I didn't have was
                                                            irrelevant.

Maybe Caroline didn't know if she was deprived either
because it's not memory, but childhood that fails to know, to measure
as even decades are unable, the protean, accidental fabric.

ENVY

Envy is a fantasy about everyone else
often misplaced or, time will tell...

I've always said, I got my father's legs
and my mother's insanity

neither of which is a good thing.
Sometimes, every day is a bad hair day.

Then there are utter mountains
of good luck. Is it immoral to be happy?

Or, in this terrible age
a moral imperative?

Is that why they follow me—
these feelings of abashment—

and, I want to call my autobiography
Nowhere Between Guilt and Envy

which I don't really mean to be funny
and doubtless will never be written?

FOR WILLIAM VON EGGERS DOERING (1917-2011)
PROFESSOR OF CHEMISTRY

It was only poetry I wanted to learn—
few enough words to actually read
and density for the effort.
Until I found him in the dovecote dead of the needless efforts.—W.S. Merwin

Something durable, although we know nothing is truly.
Why do we keep expecting life to be easy, when we know it never can be?
—Robert Lowell

Less and less it seems.
The great leveler, life, is an intractable steamroller.
Life is a great leveler—James Wright, at his last poetry reading.

Insatiable echoes! Is allusion mother or cannibal?

And yet, tones and phrases ring clear
as the squealing swifts that surround the chimneys.

No wisdom here, or only the wish
that wisdom not be this knowledge:

We live among the dead
turning each over and over
like coins from foreign countries.

GARDENER

The work of the garden
the stinking weeds
and some do stink—
those pretty early spring
onion flowers
spreading like gossip.

And the worst—*bindweed*—
masquerading as morning glory
but with python capacities.
I may have actually planted it
from a packet with Chinese writing
that came as a party favor.

Certainly the roots of all evil—
white and sinewy
plump as boiled bucatini
even in winter, burrowing
for all I know all the way
to China.

Moments of astonishment
and panic overtook me—
early spring, and nothing else
was growing.

The internet suggested
abandoning the property.

But, entrepreneurship pinged—
perhaps they're edible, succulent
the newest trendy vegetable, maybe
even medicinal, heroic...

(How often have I wished
for a humanitarian use
for poison ivy?)

I would say I was a like surgeon
painstakingly excising tumors
though a better analogy
would be Medusa's hairdresser.

But, there was a meditative quality, too
a zone of satisfaction ignited
or honed by insistence.
I could be hateful to the core
without guilt or remorse.
The redundancy suited my obsessionality.
I was out there
in the early spring sun, flared nostrils
breathing unheard-of delight
in faint wood smoke.
One, then the other, cat came
to be with me. I was
out there for a long time
dirty and on my knees
authentically engaged
in thankless
honest
labor.

GROWING OLD

You have to understand
I didn't ask for this—
Neither the sunspots
nor midgeted future.

Or memory, migrating like ink
on wet watercolor paper.

Ignored because we're dotty
even if we're not.

Not as gentle as *wearing purple*
no such liberation in rebellion.
I'm squally and selfish, feckless.
There, I've used *feckless* in a poem.
Feck you!

Memory fading beyond retrieval
or concern, even beyond
narcissistic injury. It will happen
to you, too.

*

I am an old woman.
How old is that?
Am I old enough to chose
where I want to die?

Does anyone get to?
If you go somewhere and
stay put, you have a chance
a certain chance.

In France, I say.
How un-American.
In fantasy, please
where else?

In a castle, or near one
or near a ruined one.
They abound.
It's assured!

*

I can't be afraid of life
because of death
(and neither can you).

I like it here.
What I don't like is the world
where *the glass knights*
lie by their gloves of blood.

Or the intrusion
of unbidden, unwanted
dread. Sorrow

is expected, a vagrant wind.
Expect it eventually
but not now.

You, beautiful friend
more than one
or my ever-dying
husband

(not exactly or really, I'm just
precocious in my worry).

And, don't think worry
doesn't ward off
(*write it!*) ...*disaster.*
Hey, but it doesn't.

*

As a young child I asked my father
"Does it help to pray?"
He said, "If it makes you feel better
then it helps to pray."
A generous atheist's open-ended
lesson to a child.

So now, genetic or otherwise
nurtured nature
I have atheist prayers
and they're needed
more and more
and not so many *miles to go.*

*

Regret? No.
For what?

We've tried to fulfill our dreams
now let us fulfill our realities.

I am an old woman
mournful and fierce.

No song will ever be sung
that isn't a dirge.

I Hate Money

I hate having it
and not having it.
I hate having too much
and having too little, especially.
(...nowhere between guilt and envy.)

Not that I'm starving
not by a long shot.
I'm almost rich enough
to be thin, but do you know
how obscene money is?

It brands and scars our would-be
kind souls that might have said
I want to live at least quietly
if not to do and be for others.

Do you know how humiliating and corrupt?
I say this having lived at the bottom
and among the top, counting summers by numbers
of open oyster bars, slurping until my ankles
were swollen from the salt. And, I can tell you
truly, the rich are no happier than anyone else.

...how corrosive money really is?
abhorrent, abominable, appalling, atrocious, disgusting,
dreadful, foul, ghastly, grotesque,
heinous, hideous, loathsome, monstrous, nauseating, odious,
repugnant, repulsive, revolting, vile
The thesaurus is not plump enough.

Are you rich enough for philanthropy
to preen before the mirror of your gifts?
(Clever those development officers.)
How much is enough

enough enough enough?
I hate the euro and the pound
ditto the rupee, ruble and yen
doubloons and wampum too.
Not a nickel of value to be had.

But, most of all
I hate the almighty dollar
for taking a living dream
from looking like a nice snake
who swallowed a mouse in its middle
to one that swallowed a pimple and a balloon.

*

A patient once came to me from the ghetto—not sure
how he got to my rather tony street all of a few blocks away.
More than one person in the neighborhood said
"A guy in a do-rag was hanging around your office."
He had a disability for which he certainly could have collected.
But, he wanted to work, and did for many years until
his job was eliminated by some corporate whatever.
Only then did he claim his benefits, and something
of a retro windfall, about ten grand, I think. He gave $1,000 each
to his mother, father, sister, and brother. He bought himself
a couple pairs of sneakers, matching t-shirts and do-rags.
(He couldn't think of anything else he wanted—how blessed is that?)
But then, others appeared—neighbors and friends, cousins (1st,
2nd, and 3rd), former colleagues and classmates, hospitals
drug addicts and clergy, benevolent (we hope) police, boy and girl
scouts, musicians, sports teams and librarians, all with their hands out.
He was amused if not bewildered, at least a bit annoyed and said
what still chimes in my head like the exegesis of an ancient text:
Ya know doc, money is funny.
(And to those who complain about athletes taking the knee
I want to say, *kneeling is a lot like praying.*)

I Will Always Have the Sky

At a young age I can't quite guess—
perhaps five or six—
I remember being at what we called
the big park. Yes, in contrast to
the little park down the hill.

The little park had benches
and a sandbox, maybe a water fountain
but nothing else. It was just for sitting
maybe with the dog, and was next to the woods
where we went sledding
when we were older.

The big park had see-saws and swings
a sprinkler and a jungle gym. Once
a girl in a bathing suit, wet from the sprinkler
swinging upside down, fell on her head.
Mothers leapt instantaneously.
I still wonder what happened to her
sometimes.

(Another girl, a friend, crashed her sled.
The mothers leapt again.
One put snow on her cheek
to stop the bleeding.)

I remember being at the edge
of the big park, looking out onto a meadow
which was actually just a big lawn.
(I don't think I saw a proper meadow
until many years later.)

I looked at the sky, which was bright blue
that day with big puffy white clouds—
cheery and pretty. I remember thinking:
Wherever I am the sky will be there.
Whatever happens, I will always have the sky.

I don't know how to account
for this preternatural philosophical moment.
I remember it as a comforting, happy revelation.
As yet unaware *the best things in life are free*
perhaps it was some kind of nascent pride
in scientific mastery.

Unlike the pentimenti of injured children
and beyond the abiding beauty of the sky itself
I do not know what intensity of emotion
encoded that moment, what if any trauma

or was it merely the life force—*élan vital*—
behind a lifelong certainty.

I will always have the sky.
(And you will too.)

In the Cave

There I was
and it collapsed.
There I was, unharmed
but trapped. I thought
here I am
about to die a miserable death
of dehydration and fear.

Immobile, but I could scratch
an itch. Imagine
if it had been otherwise.

I had a few hours left
or so I thought
and so I thought
of all I loved, and sorrow
and how they blended into
an unmistakable *ache.*

Such a trite word
yet it embodies the world
and beyond. All longing
all despair, the tenderness
of an injury healing, or the ominous
decree that it won't.

And, so the sky had fallen
so to speak, the limestone sky
and there was darkness.
There were no shadows
but there still was air.

There were metaphors
but really, who cares?

For a while I sang
badly, as ever, but disturbing
no one—

Down yonder green valleys...

It was consoling—
the way I used to sing
to the little black kitten—
chaton noir—
who was gravely ill.

In the Cave Redux

So, there I really was
driving by troglodyte dwellings in rural France—
or my husband was driving because I drive
as badly as I sing—in the darkest mood
because the damn feral kitten whom I unexpectedly
loved more than life itself turned out to be FIV+
and I didn't yet know it wasn't as bad as I thought.

So, I jotted down a gloomy, allegorical poem.
You have to understand, we were in the middle
of nowhere. But, suddenly, a familiar font
flashed across the pastoral landscape—
PF DIN Text Pro Light or family
I've since learned along with
something about cat viruses.

What? Wait, go back!

Moments later, there I was
squealing with obscene delight—
Magasin D'Usine Chaussures—
in the factory outlet store
of my favorite brand of shoes
of which I'd only ever owned one used pair
next to the factory itself no less.
Oh, I might have loved to see the interior
though hopefully not as much as I loved
the precipitously forgotten kitten.

I started to say, *The moral of the story is...*
but, morality has little purchase here—perhaps
little to do with human nature at all.

So, *the point of the story is*
we are all parfaits of selves
with shifting layers, some of them rambling, each
as authentic or inauthentic as the other
at any dolorous, randomly given moment.

JOHANNA

I had lunch in a Tibetan restaurant
at ten o'clock in the morning
waiting to see you.

You were
gracious, of course
even to the klutzy kid Rabbi.

So, how's everything going today?

Far more gracious than I'd have been.
I'd have bitten his head off.
Why not?

Gracious under blankets, afraid
only of pain, which everyone promised
would not come.

"Maybe it doesn't matter," you said
and I thought I knew
what you meant.

But, now I'm not sure.
Was I arrogant in knowing—
prescient beyond understanding

what I couldn't possibly
have understood?
Maybe it doesn't matter.

How quietly you spoke
though you were never loud.
And, how we embraced

not fading, but anticipatory fading
with particular intent
to remember while we could:

the luxury of Paris—that day trip
to Chartres, the photograph
of you walking away

after years
of implacable insistence.
Maybe it doesn't matter.

MOZART REQUIEM

I'm sitting in a church
on a very hard bench
narrow, with no back
listening to Mozart's Requiem—
a very large, very old church
in France, overflowing
with the choir's *noir*
the listeners' silence—
two and a quarter centuries later
and not a day.

What music
invents the brain, releases it
as if we're sentient to be nothing
but creatures of grief
and ecstasy?

What dream rests
on what precipice
of what dream?

＊

Let me tell you what I know.
You will search for your life
and then it will be over.
The search is the only.

Don't be docile
or smug. Being *yourself*
is not always a good idea.
Try to modulate
with auxiliary ballast
and gravitas.

If you come from trauma
large or small (don't we all?)
then heal as best you're able.
Better yet, help others
heal.

Touch the velvet of crows
far across the field, sing
their suspended melancholy

as if nature was not unkind
as if human nature, in particular
was not unkind.

*

The yards of hair
of old women
are tied behind them, their heads
nodding but still upright.

I can no longer
subtract my years from theirs
and find many left.

The end of immortality is clear.

I'm no longer arrogant enough
to feel sorry for them
but have begun to fear
the labor of their hair.

*

Music of centuries
but millennia of stone
carved and carried
how?

Even an atheist can see
God must be
this ability.

A daughter is tending an agèd mother
a child is sitting on a lap
or an animal is.

Renascence, Recuerdo
palpable
in the last forgotten universe.

My Grandmother's Ring

I didn't know her. I never met her.
She died before I was born.
I hadn't even heard many stories about her
except that she pinched my father under the dinner table
for talking with his mouth full, or such
and was a bit of a stage mother.

Her favorite son (my father, of course)
was the next Caruso, except he wasn't.
(Nothing like an angelic pre-adolescent voice
changing to 'pleasant'.)

I have two photographs, one of which might be of her.
One is of a handsome, dignified woman
but the one I'd always thought
is not—not even plain—gawky, downright homely
(duly noted with feminist chagrin).
There's no way to tell who or whom
and no one left to tell.

She shows up in the 1940 census
as living in Chicago with my parents.
(Or were they, as my husband rudely asks
though it never occurred to me, living with her?
How often was a woman 'head of household' back then?)

But, it hardly matters. Ancestors, after all
are about fantasy, aren't they?

At a certain age, OK, sixty
I decided to put on her wedding ring.
It, I'd always known, was hers—

big and narrow, platinum, with a row of diamond fragments
a bit of decorative incising, quite worn and wobbly.

Not like the other grandmother's—a simple gold band
barely a five, the toxic ring, never even
tried on (even if I could)—the suicide.

I wear the too-large circle inside my own
(plus the little antique store diamond
from someone else's ancestor).
I imagine she may help me, specifically, with speaking up.

Speak up, but not too, too much
neither without gratitude nor abhorrence
for what we've wrought, the too many multitudes
of us—leaving animals with no quiet land
to rest on, or water to swim in, or skin.

My articulate grandmother! After all
ancestors are about fantasy—after all
they and we—*poor passing facts.*

ON WRITING

The full thrust is there
behind the pause—
pause for emphasis or, to listen.

How to get the inside out
to tell the truth as if there is
such a thing.

How to fall in love with a word—*authenticity*—
without the vanity of polishing it.

Years ago, I started reading Rilke
each translation better or worse
than the last and the next
each line, tone, affectation
a word here, a word there

all inadequate.

So many hours of so many psychic translators
I started to feel the angels winging
straight through the German
through the atmosphere of stratosphere—
a man who wrote in French before his death—

right through the words, as if
they were already neuronal, merely
neuronal, abundant, ticking, awry.

I felt those angels.
There were no words.

ONCE IN FRANCE

Once I wrote a poem (which I can't find
but will continue to look for) that began
Once, in France, I tasted a potato.

The famous poet at the famous university
hated it. I mean *hated*, ridiculed
beyond any possibility of what an erudite man
(he happened to be a man) would allow.

And I say, these decades later
he missed the point.

Once, in France, I tasted a potato.
You have to understand, *I tasted* it. First, it *had* a taste
unlike those bland and bloated American spuds
or every other vegetable upsized and de-scented.

I was young and afraid to cross the street
in front of my own house so crossed the ocean instead
and tasted the miracle of France, a place as far away
from starchy homogenization as *mer et ciel*—
sea and sky themselves. You have no idea how far.

Should we have stayed at home and thought of here?

Or is one inescapably home, the globe merely
incidental to an inner life, or an inner, inner life
rejoicing in flavor unknown to travelers
jubilant with conviction that what I know is real
and true still—the beauty of the world a different
kind of flavor, or the imagination, full.

Cool meadows, castles beyond. Only running
toward an edge of fantasy can make ecstasy.
Or the potato itself, 10,000 years and 1,000 varieties
indigenous to the Andes—indígena, indigène—
conveying secrets inconceivable at home.
The world is always larger.

I want neither to reify nor import it
annoyed now as I wasn't then
by his contempt, but to peel away
the queasy self-conscious young woman
filled with longing for the tongue's love
beyond the parsing of words.

ONCE UPON A TIME

It's for one's older age
to write lightly, nothing terribly serious
anymore, if there ever was. Of course
there was, and is, but I mean
fervent, or what I really mean
is *hysterical*. Not so much need anymore
if there ever was.

I asked my friend Roberta, a generation older
after her friend Sylvia died, yet another friend.
How do you deal with all the death? She said
It becomes muted. Somehow
it becomes muted.

And, I think once more of Rilke writing in French
before his death—vignettes. What could be
greater proof of *légèreté?*

In any event, there's also a freedom
to meander like a river that never wanted
to course directly, and so:

Once upon a time when I was a medical student
I traipsed and trailed along with the team
in and out of patients' rooms. *Good morning
how are you feeling today?*—cheerful, well-intentioned
more than a little perfunctory, a name here
there, another, and the next: Warren, R.

He had papers around his bed.
I'm well, thank you, he said or, I forget. And, I forget
if I left the room and then spun back, or not
but what I remember was seeing something
iridescent about him, and shouting
You're Robert Penn Warren!

What I saw was his glass eye, ordinary Mr. Warren
transformed, sitting amidst papers, of course.
And, I believe he must have said, *Yes,* of course.
Maybe he smiled.

So now thirty odd years later
I've violated confidentiality.
No one else on the team
had ever heard of him...

Let me meander again to say
however fervent you may be
you are light, and you are muted
or will be.

I remember asking his permission to return
and came back later, short white coat and all.
I sat at his bedside, and forget what I said—
that I liked/read/wrote poetry.

He was gracious, like a teacher, or a mentor—
all I imagined a poet to be. And, what he said
what I remember a not-too-ill old man
surrounded by papers saying, in retrospect
with more than a little admonishment:

It's a full-time job.

PHOTOGRAPHING THE DAISY FIELD

The daisy field.
I love the orderliness. I love
the chaos.

Oh shit, I nuked them!

I'm waiting for June to come
again. I think they come
in June.

Need a cloudy day.
Good.

What are those other yellow things?

Should I ask permission?
OK, the owner was nice
said they call it
the daisy field.

He liked my dog
(who is not in the photos).

Chaotic, beautiful.
The wind is blowing—is that OK?
Pointillism?

Scotch broom is pretty too, but invasive.

Focus! How come nothing's in focus?
Where's the dog?
Please don't think or say *Monet.*

POEMS ARE LIKE

Poems are like visitations
truly, they visit upon you
especially after a glass of wine, or two.
Then you have to read 'em
to see what they say
and fix them, so they make
any sense at all

if you care (I do, mostly)
or otherwise say they've arrived
full-blown from the head of Zeus.

But really, they're from a whole life
or a moment of life—even youth
has something to say
or can't help saying.

And, they're like the reflection
of the brass eBay chandelier
in the modest poster frame
reframed with homemade art—
accidental and cherished.

Poetry comes from a far away place
not entirely desolate, no, but not
the whole story either, not quite
the totally silly or pedestrian, not
the bourgeois, *heavens no!*

PSYCHOANALYSIS

A silly thing, really
to lie on a couch—
rather stylized.

Why not in a meadow
in the arms of a lover
or leaning gently
on a favorite member of the flock—
pastoral?

But, the thoughts
weren't silly—often painful
if redundant.

One's story is one's own
is one's universe.

The analyst was kind.
He had a day job
of great importance

yet was willing to sit
predawn practically
and listen to me
(for a fee)

almost daily
for all eternity.

You're being so nice
I said. He said
I'm not being nice
I'm just being.

I'm reminded now, somehow
of a stray kitten I took in
who couldn't decide
between food and affection.

Now now, he said
sometimes, when I went
on and on.

Once he reached over
and touched my head.

When the holidays came
I had five places to go—
You have more friends than I do, he said—
but, I wanted none. None
was family, none
was home, none
was my own.

Once, on the subject
of finding true love
he even said
If you want to make an omelet
you have to break some eggs.

Occasionally, I looked
around the room
as much as I could
without leaning too far—
a few knickknacks, Asian
or African, *de rigueur* perhaps.

Once I sat up, and looked at him.
I was in the middle
of a complaint, OK
a bit of a tirade.

(Perhaps, kindly, he'd say
it was a *lament*.)

And, all I saw
was an old man
with a rubbery face
benign as apples, very slightly
quizzical, sitting patiently.

One mentor said
*The neurosis eventually
kind of burns itself out.*
How un-profound
for all that style.

Is that what happened?

One day, or some days, eternity
came to an end. I knew
it was time to go.
I wasn't happy about leaving
but willing.

Not too long after
I moved into a house
not too far away—
a very nice house.

Psychoanalysis had cured me
of orphanhood.

Rage

I cannot find
the luminous mountain.

Where where where

amid a core of hate
too primitive for corruption or deceit—

Just pure burning, the molten, useless
revenge of a child's tantrum, that child
wholly sincere in the desire
to blow up the universe.

That child, loved or un-loved, fed or not
blistered, wandering, desolate.

A species problem—and, we're all at risk
of going to the same nowhere.

RETIREMENT

And, so I faded out quietly—
retirement by default I like to say, but it was
shocking never the less
as it became so.

No medals or toasts, perhaps envy
if I'd have told anyone
or supreme panic...

Envy for wealth? Envy away—
I've counted every nickel
to the grave.

Please don't make me rhyme
but yes, they *fade*—
purpose, identity, influence
skin tone, balance, and dearest of all
memory
all fade.

I'm looking for redemption in wisdom
(when the wise are merely grateful
for a roof over their heads).

But, what I find
are a few herbs, feathery chervil, even
a stray cat, grateful as if
at the breast of a Madonna
and that is enough.

And, so I've waited all my life
for this—an adolescent fantasy of being
free enough to lunch everyday
at the Horn and Hardart on 86th
with dear friends.

How fun it would have been
if it existed—those beautiful brass
deco cubby-holes—or
if the friends existed

if I was still an urbanite and not
decades, chapters, and continents away
free at last of having to be

anything when I grow up.

RUMINATION

I want her to her think I'm not
worried about $ between us
because among friends...

I don't want her to be insulted
because I'm not concerned about $
and she is (though she's rich.)

I don't want her to think I feel
too guilty for getting too good
a deal because then she'll feel
badly for getting a bad deal.

She must be the one to feel
generous without feeling
like a chump!

SEEKING THE PLACE OF POETRY

A small room
of childhood, or a dream
or a dream of childhood.

The absence of the corporeal
or just the essence
of a body, the sensations.

Time is in abeyance. Memory fades
or sharpens uselessly.
No argument, no commentary.

There was a time
when I didn't sway.

Now, everything makes
my whole unreal body tremble.

The warm and the ever
the word and the oar

reedy sleep, the afghan hunter
bug runs the corner of my eye

cascade, as if thought—
thought as if
sense.

What is the difference
between childhood and a dream?

(Don't mock me!)

Sometimes I Want...

...to cry
and cry. Hard to tell
if it's sorrow or joy
relief or awe
a vagrant post-menopausal hormone storm
or my mother's bad bipolar genes.

Sometimes I feel
I'm nearly ready
to be free.

How much time, and how much regret
equals the evanescent freedom
for which tears are all
of the above?

SPEAKING FRENCH

Not a lot of words are needed
especially with the old women.
Something happens
pointing to the flowers
a noun or two, a gesture, a verb
infinitive only, who cares

and we're kissing each other
easily—*bisous!*

Ca va? is the question
of the day, every day.
Whose day is without
the importance and generosity
of this question? Whose day
needs more, really?

Sans discours as I know (and love) it
but the tenderness grows—
a grandchild's age, a small complaint
perhaps barely grasped, the weather
of course.

(For deeper conversation
I talk all day to the plants.)

We sit in the same world
of brick and stone, *ancien,* tall
trees swaying in the near distance.
We know the village by heart
every *pavé,* we know the cats

who make the rounds
and the miracle of affection.

Step Out of Your Life

Step out of your life.
There's a great deal of illusion:

Is the fabric what you do, or what you think
what you believe in, or who believes you?

Is it what you cook?—the labor
sustenance, or fluff?

Your children, yes, though neither always
nor entirely.

What is freedom and what is sloth
or exile?

A mentor (of sorts)
who, by the way, was having a 3rd child

at 55 because he knew he'd lose one
in the war, once said

It doesn't matter what you commit yourself to
as long as you commit yourself to something.

What is freedom?
Ask again.

Inconsequence.

THE CASTLE

It crumbles slowly
imperceptibly, as do our hearts.
A ruined castle is still

a castle, or is it?
They're hard to ruin.
It takes centuries.

I want to go and be
with the shabbiness, a place
where time goes nowhere—

fine clouds of summer
willing to block the sun
now and then, just enough

against the blue to cool—
a life of small savor
a momentary kind

of ecstasy. Let me sink
to where I belong
but no lower.

How graced I am
not to drown—
just a thread of dawdling—

Wait. Let me rest.
Not to rush
life in one's head

is bliss.
I am here to sink
like a floating stone.

The wind plays the tall chimneys like flutes
the mailbox flaps, and then
there are the maddening doves—

Whoo whoo WHOO
Whoo whoo WHOO
Whoo whoo WHOO

In the end we know
there are no heroes
but there is love.

The world is crumbling.
Has it always been?

THE DEAD PROFESSOR'S BOOKS

The dead professor's books
sit stalwart and important, *snug* too—
(a comforting word, suiting books).

Why do we wrap ourselves in them
(or used to, before the internet), enshrine
though not necessarily
read—

Austen, Bakhtin, Conrad, Dostoyevsky, Foucault
on a lovely wooden shelf.

I put them there, in all fairness
knowing he was ill—
(I might otherwise have selectively
de-accessioned)—

and felt sad—the emblem
of a man, a nice man
of a scholar, of scholarship
I looked up and bowed down
to.

(Hardly anyone does these days.)

It is a goodbye
and I goodbye I refuse to say.

The Elderly Couple

They died
in their 90's, each within weeks
of the other. They were
in their day *a tour de force*
in their way.

They died healthy
one in sleep, one
I'm not sure, but quickly.
No children by their sides
but healthy and wealthy
at least somewhat
and wise, perhaps.

I don't know where
they came from
or where their decades went.
They entertained each other
royally, and others
with letters to the editor.

(I do not mean
to be dismissive or unkind
but only to say
with more or less fanfare
we are all
going their way.)

THE GOLDFISH POND

Sundays, inside the iron gates
I watched them swim—
great flashes of gold beneath murky water.

My father brought Hershey bars, and cigarettes.
The narrow balconies looked like cages—
Victorian ironwork against dark red brick

latticed respite from the heat
like an aviary. Ah, the 50's
when *lunacy* was still an acceptable word.

Hershey bars with almonds, always.
My father was patient and kind.
"You will never know her as I did." he said.

Seven thousand alit those balconies.
Children were not allowed.
My father left me at the goldfish pond.

She didn't find them unkind.
I've read the records—thorough, substantive
not unkind.

They stole from her though
all her turquoise from the Southwest
all the memories from when she was six

before there was kinder electricity
or maybe she just gave the old pawn away.
I liked watching the goldfish.

I am also behind locked doors.
I carry the keys—how light they are
jingling like jewelry—

but will never know
how deliriously safe and comforted
she felt within those walls.

One day, it started to rain on the goldfish.
The drops never touched them
swimming deeply in their dark pond.

THE HONESTY OF DISPASSION

More and more a little threnody—
Old age suits me.
Senescence (of all things)
equals serenity.

I got rich
(no, not very rich)
and bought a house in France—
five stories of stone
and here I sit

deprived of all but sky.

These are not melancholy thoughts.
They're comforting in their authenticity.

I've climbed almost every mountain
I've wanted to climb
moral compass intact.

A new world now
is repose.

I'm sad
for us as a species
but not without joy or fun
joy and fun
much without belief
in anything, really
except what is.

How individually we live
creating reality willy-nilly
with such conviction
it is.

THINKING OF BIRDS

Thinking of all the birds
whose flight has been bred out of them
or managed by civilization, those barbequed
or eaten by feral cats.

No bleeding heart I
but meant to soar, longing
somehow to soar
high enough to see the roofs
not my friends below
but carrion.

They're not always pleasant
beings with wings.
But, they can fly!

This House

The woman of this house
is rapt, staring into the ferns.
My Queendom! Ha—far from Queens!
Not enough hours in a lifetime
for gratitude. Don't you see
I just need to bleat and bleat
my relief, though never a moment
without the fear of loss.
This house, I'm your
slave to every splinter–
...deserve you...deserve you not...

THOSE OLD GRAMMARIANS

Those old grammarians—
why we loved them, or do now
for the order—*seder*—sown.

Not *none are...*
None is *not one.* None *is...*
Not *the data is...* A datum *is...*
The data *are...*

Authoritative and authoritarian.

I was still practically a teenager
reading William Safire—
a Republican no less (who knew?)—
for perverse delight.

All those rules, practically a secret society
comforting as the last sovereignty
of a *GOMER*†.

Language dances in my head like swifts
whistling across the chimney pots, flutes
mixed metaphors crashing like waves
crystal, china, porcelain, glass
rioting in the thesaurus.

*

Once, while I was on vacation
a nice neighbor agreed
to water the plants.

"They can't be over-watered," I said
meaning, *Don't worry about over-watering them
because the water pours right through.*

They can't be over-watered, I said
dumb as the plants
that or which all died of thirst.

Small potatoes *that* and *which,* but
why why why do you call me a *that*
when I'm a *who?*

All those words—what will be your
thunderous last?

                    *

And yet a poem
cannot be 'written', cannot abide
intentionality, but is invoked
from a thud or a rush, a manic thunderbolt
the blood jet, a wisp chaliced
from and to oblivion.

†Get Out of My Emergency Room

Time Passes

Time passes without apology, or remorse.
Of course *time* can't *apologize*.

But, you think it should, or might.
Just something other than relentlessness—

Something to adjudicate the expectation
of spring coming, then summer.

The grass is high, really high, untended.
It's not my grass though.

It will be cut, or not. I will cut it
or not, and it matters not

or not very much. Then it will be straw-like.
See what I mean, *relentless*.

And it matters so much
that every molecule in the universe

cries with remorse
for the stupidity of the weeping universe.

TIMES ONE NEEDS

Times one needs to contemplate
the troubles of the world
to sit, in the last light of paradise
on a crooked bench
in an emerald lawn, and all that
and wash the sorrow

of a boy so enraged his heart
erupted at an untold moment
into nonsensical silence.

a woman who holds the universe
together with the very certainty
that it cannot be held together
that it cannot be held

one who blathers, and sighs
one who writes poetry
where none is called for

and writes and writes
until the sirens and the doctors
insist on returning her
to the other maze.

Truly, the bench is crooked
from neglect, but deliberately, too
roughhewn from the start.
Lichen and grain make it beautiful
beyond all imagining.

And, the far trees
not yet entirely in bloom—
impossibly huge for sandy land.

They're a different kind
of contemplation. Their sorrow
is mute, their violence borne
only in their majesty.

They create me
as did the furious child.

Am I so easily created?

TRUE LOVE

When my analyst commented
I was dwelling on the past

I said (thinking I was paraphrasing Freud)
"The past echoes." He said
"Then why can't you hear it
as *echoes?*"

It's worth
letting one's very important
central narrative, truth-be-told
as you're sticking to it
not
be all of life.

I was a lonely hearts girl
for a long time (forgive *girl*
it's colloquial and re-claimed).

And, I've met many—hard
not to feel flawed, internalize toxic
have-not, unwanted, unlovable
mishegas.

"Am I doing something wrong?" I asked.
"Of course you're doing something wrong." he said.

I did find true love
after kissing a few frogs, or snakes
but none for very long
or, even they wouldn't have me.

Finally, instead of trying to heal
my mother, I married my father
Oedipal guilt be damned!

And, as my mother had said
Here is a man who will never hurt me.

True love, ordinary as pie
in some extraordinary universe.

Where were you all those years?

(Probably a few possibilities if one has
one's eyes open, antennae screwed on right
isn't guilty, sabotaging, terrified—
unconsciously of course—and wasting time
kissing amphibians and reptiles.)

I still have dreams
that I'm a lonely hearts girl
with some frequency and misery—
recapitulation of one heartbreak
or another—trying and trying.

I wake up and have to breathe
the sweat away and remember
my husband exists and I'm safely

loved for decades now, safe
and yet the recrudescent
dreams of trauma, safe

until death do we part.

VILLANELLE

OK, I've had enough.
I need time
and will not be rushed.

I'll take as long as I want just
to watch a snail leave a trace of slime.
I need enough

for devotion to tortuous form, to hush
psychotic clang erupting from endless rhyme.
Some things cannot be rushed.

I've mastered *the art of losing,* trust
me, and *going gentle* will be just fine
preferable, actually, but truly I've had enough

and never again will be pushed
to prematurely pluck a vine.
What's the rush?

Wait until those languid grapes are in full blush!
Lollygaging all the way would be divine.
There will never be enough...
I hope I won't be rushed.

YOU'RE ALLOWED TO LOVE

You're allowed to love
what you love.
Indeed, who can help loving
what they love, or whom
even if unpopular—
when everyone loves The Beatles
and your favorite group
is The Vienna Choir Boys.
Go figure. Go fish.
You're allowed to love
old brick and stone
the townie bar, the craggy garden
the smelly mutt, too many memories
ghosts of love, icons that never fell
and those loved all the more
because they did.
Deckle edges, hedges, clang
associations (look it up)
faded linen, rumpled too
kitties and puppies even more
than normal folks do
curve and cusp
remembrance–like *embrace*–words
as if without utterance
the fantasy of a kingdom
or a mother or father
always beyond reach.

NOTES ON THE POEMS:

An Æsthetic of Stone, page 3, last 2 lines, *...or by lips/on the foot of a saint.* – allusion to the statue of St. Peter in Vatican City by Arnolfo di Cambio, c.1300.

As If, page 5, line 6, *Are you nobody, too?* Emily Dickinson.

for William von Eggers Doering, page 12, line 4, *Until I found him in the dovecote dead of the needless efforts.* – W.S. Merwin, *Fly*; line 6, *Why do we keep expecting life to be easy, when we know it never can be?* – Robert Lowell, *To Mother*; line 10, *Life is a great leveler.* – James Wright, overheard at his last reading, Cambridge, MA, October 1979.

Growing Old, page 15, line 9, *...wearing purple*, allusion to Jenny Joseph, *Warning*; page 16, lines 14 & 15, *The glass knights lie by their gloves of blood.* – W.S. Merwin, *I Live Up Here*; page 17, line 4, *(write it!) ...disaster* – allusion to Elizabeth Bishop, *One Art*; line 17, *miles to go* – allusion to Robert Frost, *Stopping by Woods on a Snowy Evening*.

I Hate Money, page 19, last line, *kneeling is a lot like praying* – allusion to M.L. King 1965 and Colin Kaepernick & others 2016.

I Will Always Have the Sky, page 21, line 9, *the best things in life are free* – Buddy DeSylva & Lew Brown, lyrics, 1927.

In the Cave, page 23, line 4, *Down Yonder Green Valleys... "The Ash Grove"*, Welsh Folk Song.

Mozart Requiem, page 28, lines 16-18, *What dream rests/on what precipice/of what dream?* – allusion to Edgar Allen Poe, *A Dream Within A Dream*; page 30, line 11, *Renascence, Recuerdo* – allusion to Edna St. Vincent Millay.

My Grandmother's Ring, page 32, last line, *poor passing facts.* Robert Lowell, *Epilogue*.

Once in France, page 34, line 19, *Should we have stayed at home and thought of here?* Elizabeth Bishop, *Questions of Travel*.

Those Old Grammarians, page 60, line15, and page 61, footnote, *GOMER* = *Get Out of My Emergency Room*, Samuel Shem, "The House of God", page 61, line 13, *the blood jet*, Sylvia Plath, *Kindness.*

Villanelle, page 67, line 10, *the art of losing*, Elizabeth Bishop, *One Art;* line 11, *going gentle* – allusion to Dylan Thomas, *Do not go gentle into that good night.*

LAURI ROBERTSON has written poetry for many years—Adrienne Rich was her mentor. She is a psychiatrist/psychoanalyst formerly on the clinical faculty of Yale Medical School. She's also a fine art photographer, represented on Nantucket Island by The Gallery at Four India: laurirobertsonphotography.com. *An Æsthetic of Stone* is inspired by life in rural France.